Timely Tasks
for
Fast Finishers

5–7 Year Olds

Peter Clutterbuck

Brilliant Publications

We hope you and your pupils enjoy using this book. You might be interested in these other books published by Brilliant Publications:

Timely Tasks: 7–9 Year Olds   978-1-905780-01-3
Timely Tasks: 9–11 Year Olds   978-1-905780-02-0
Brilliant Activities for Gifted and Talented Children   978-1-903853-47-4
Thinking Strategies for the Successful Classroom: 5–7 Year Olds   978-1-905780-03-7
Thinking Strategies for the Successful Classroom: 7–9 Year Olds   978-1-905780-04-4
Thinking Strategies for the Successful Classroom: 9–11 Year Olds   978-1-905780-05-1

If you would like further information on these or other titles published by Brilliant Publications, please look at our website www.brilliantpublications.co.uk or write to the address below.

Published in the UK by Brilliant Publications

Sales:

BEBC (Brilliant Publications)
Albion Close, Parkstone, Poole, Dorset BH12 3LL
Tel: 0845 1309200   01202 712910
Fax: 0845 1309300
e-mail: brilliant@bebc.co.uk
website: www.brilliantpublications.co.uk

Editorial and Marketing:

10 Church View, Sparrow Hall Farm, Edlesborough, Dunstable,
Bedfordshire LU6 2ES
Tel: 01525 222292

The name Brilliant Publications and its logo are registered trademarks.

Written by Peter Clutterbuck
Typeset and designed by Bob Reyes
Illustrations by Greg Anderson-Clift
Cover by Lynda Murray
Text copyright © Peter Clutterbuck 2001
© 2001 BLAKE PUBLISHING

This edition is for sale in the United Kingdom only. Originally published in Australia by Blake Publishing.

ISBN 978-1-905780-00-6

Printed 2007 in the UK
10   9   8   7   6   5   4   3   2   1

CONTENTS

Task Cards

Make a word

Make words to match the pictures. Use one letter from each box.

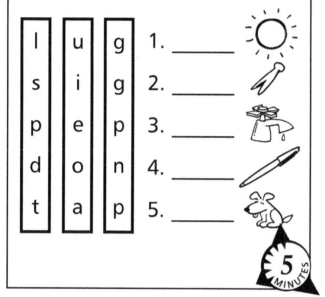

l	u	g
s	i	g
p	e	p
d	o	n
t	a	p

1. _____
2. _____
3. _____
4. _____
5. _____

Change the order

Change the order of the letters to make the word to match each picture.

tar____   ram____   pat____

was____   net____   tan____

10

Little words

Find a little word in each of the big words and write it on the line below. Then draw pictures of what you have found.

elephant	then	beggar	card
ant	_____	_____	_____

crater	pansy	brain	bowl
_____	_____	_____	_____

Use a separate sheet if you need more space.

Brilliant Publications

Timely Tasks for Fast Finishers 5–7 Year Olds
© Blake Publishing

Wordsearch

Find the animal names in the grid. Write them on the lines.

c	o	w	p	i	g
h	o	r	s	e	d
b	e	a	r	x	o
t	i	g	e	r	g
r	a	b	b	i	t

_____ _____

_____ _____

_____

What's there?

Look at the picture. Colour the boxes below that contain the names of things in the picture.

car	tree	bus	sails	book
cow	fence	chair	snake	tent
elephant	house	boat	table	plate
ball	fire	cup	water	rocks

ENGLISH

Fill in the gaps

Add *'ow'* in the spaces then draw a line to the picture that matches each word.

c l _ _ n

c r _ _ n

s n _ _ _

b _ _ l

t _ _ n

Picture this

Make words to match the pictures using some of the letters in the box.

n	f	x	p	b
t		m	a	o

Classifying

Write the words in the box under the correct headings below.

cake	games	pizza
shoes	butter	jumper
cricket	hat	football

 Things to eat   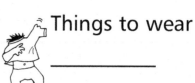 Things to play   Things to wear

_____   _____   _____

_____   _____   _____

_____   _____   _____

ENGLISH

Brilliant Publications

Timely Tasks for Fast Finishers 5–7 Year Olds

Sounds the same

Draw the missing picture.

 see	sea	 won	one
 son	sun	won... bawl	ball

Jumbled up

Unjumble the letters to find the words that match the pictures.
Write them on the lines.

1. abll

2. ntse

3. pish

_____ _____ _____

4. rtsa

5. lcko

6. mudr

_____ _____ _____

ENGLISH

Brilliant Publications

This page may be reproduced by the original purchaser for non-commercial classroom use.

Timely Tasks for Fast Finishers 5–7 Year Olds
© Blake Publishing

7

Picture this

Look at the picture, then read the sentences below. After each write YES or NO.

1. The man is cooking._____
2. A girl is sweeping the floor._____
3. A dog is lapping some milk._____
4. There are two birds in the cage._____
5. A girl is setting the table._____
6. A pot on the stove is boiling._____

5 MINUTES

Find my name

What am I?

1. My first letter is in cap but not in cat.
2. My second letter is in tig but not in tag.
3. My third letter is in log but not in lot.

I am a _____.

Draw me!

What am I?

1. My first letter is in jab but not in jam.
2. My second letter is in net but not in nut.
3. My third letter is in den but not in hen.

I am a _____.

Draw me!

Use a separate sheet if you need more space.

5 MINUTES

ENGLISH

Brilliant Publications

© Blake Publishing

Make a word

How many new words can you make by adding a letter or letters to the word *at*? You can add letters at the beginning, or the end, or both.

Write as many words as you can on the lines below. Then draw pictures of two of them in the box.

_____   _____   _____

_____   _____   _____

_____   _____

(at)

_____   _____

_____   _____   _____

_____   _____   _____

ENGLISH

Brilliant Publications

This page may be reproduced by the original purchaser for non-commercial classroom use.

Timely Tasks for Fast Finishers 5–7 Year Olds
© Blake Publishing

9

Rhyme time

Use the words in the boxes to complete each nursery rhyme.

crown after water hill

snow go went lamb

Jack and Jill went up the _____

To fetch a pail of _____

Jack fell down and broke his _____

And Jill came tumbling _____.

Mary had a little _____

Its fleece was white as _____

And everywhere that Mary _____

The lamb was sure to _____ .

Word pictures

Complete the story using words instead of pictures. Use a separate sheet to write the missing words if you need more space.

One day a _____ was swimming in the _____

when it saw a _____ and a _____ playing on the

bank. The _____ had built its _____ nearby.

In the _____ it had laid three _____. Just then

a _____ crawled out of a _____ in the ground

and so the _____ flew away.

ENGLISH

Brilliant Publications

Timely Tasks for Fast Finishers 5–7 Year Olds
© Blake Publishing

How many?

Colour *red* those boxes that contain the names of things that have *four* legs.

Colour *yellow* those boxes that contain the names of things that have only *two* legs.

chair	girl	pig	goat
boy	dog	goose	lady
hen	owl	tiger	zebra
cat	duck	man	table

5 MINUTES

Changing letters

Change the first letter in each word to make a new word that matches the picture.

| cool | hard | bear |

| bake | coat | pain |

| silk | sing | luck |

5 MINUTES

Drawing in

Look at the picture then follow the directions below.

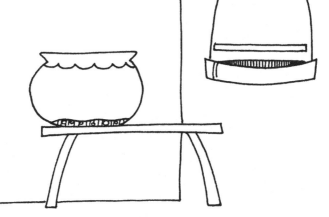

1. Draw a bird in the cage.
2. Draw three fish in the aquarium.
3. Draw a chair at the table.
4. Draw a black cat sleeping under the fish bowl.
5. Draw a clock on the wall.

5 MINUTES

ENGLISH

Brilliant Publications

This page may be reproduced by the original purchaser for non-commercial classroom use.

Timely Tasks for Fast Finishers 5–7 Year Olds

© Blake Publishing

11

Otters live near rivers in a burrow called a holt. They can swim underwater using their webbed feet and steer using their long tails. Otters are brown and live by eating fish and small animals. Only one type of otter lives in the UK.

Answer YES or NO:

1. Otters can swim underwater. _____

2. Otters don't have tails. _____

3. Otters eat fish and small animals. _____

4. Three types of otter live in the UK. _____

5. If an otter has webbed feet, colour the picture brown. If an otter does not have webbed feet, colour the picture red.

ENGLISH

Brilliant Publications

This page may be reproduced by the original purchaser for non-commercial classroom use.

Timely Tasks for Fast Finishers 5–7 Year Olds

© Blake Publishing

Which word?

Read the sentences below. Colour in the box with the correct word to complete each sentence.

1. I picked the [lamb | lemon | lolly] that was growing on the tree.

2. We can get [oil | grass | wool] from a sheep.

3. There are lots of flowers growing in the [garden | goose | postbox].

4. If you were writing a story you would use a [jelly | pencil | dog].

5. At the zoo I saw a [poor | tiger | giant].

6. You can carry water in a [bucket | fig | pony].

Crosswords

Use the picture clues across and down to complete the crosswords.

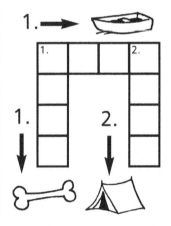

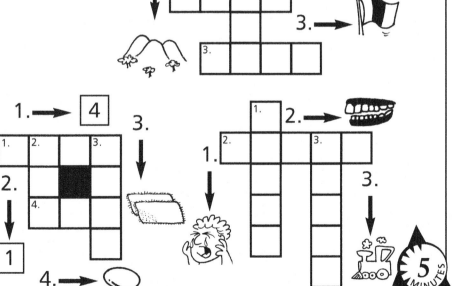

Brilliant Publications

This page may be reproduced by the original purchaser for non-commercial classroom use.

Timely Tasks for Fast Finishers 5–7 Year Olds

© Blake Publishing

13

ENGLISH

Have you ever heard a woodpecker? Woodpeckers use their long beaks to tap the bark on trees. They break bits of bark off to look behind it for insects to eat.

Woodpeckers nest in dead trees and they lay whitish eggs. They also eat seeds and nuts, and sometimes the babies and eggs that belong to other birds.

Answer *True* or *False*:

1. Woodpeckers lay whitish eggs. _____

2. Woodpeckers eat the bark from trees. _____

3. Woodpeckers build a nest of straw. _____

4. Woodpeckers sometimes eat baby birds. _____

Can you name *two* different UK birds? Write their names on the lines below, then draw pictures of them.

_____   _____

ENGLISH

Brilliant Publications

Fill in the gaps

Add 'ai' in the spaces, then draw a line to each picture that matches a word.

s __ __ l
r__ __ n
tr__ __ n
ch__ __ n
n__ __ l
t__ __ l
sn__ __ l
br__ __ n

Make it up

Use the letters in the box to make the words that match the pictures below.

x	b	f
c	o	b
u	a	d
p	t	e

_____
_____
_____
_____

Making words

Join the letter in each box to the letter pairs to make eight words.
Write the words and then draw pictures of them on a separate sheet.

1. **C**
   at
   an
   ap
   ar

   _____
   _____
   _____
   _____

2. **B**
   at
   in
   ag
   un

   _____
   _____
   _____
   _____

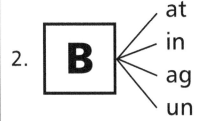

ENGLISH

Brilliant Publications

This page may be reproduced by the original purchaser for non-commercial classroom use.

Timely Tasks for Fast Finishers 5–7 Year Olds
© Blake Publishing

15

Add a letter

Add a letter to make a word that matches each picture.

 ____old

 ____tar

 ____ing

 ____rum

 ____hip

 ____lag

 ____heel

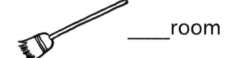 ____room

Which word?

Choose the correct word in brackets to complete each sentence. Circle it.

Tom went to the shop to buy some (**bumps milk holes**).

When we go camping we sleep in a (**box string tent**).

When babies are hungry they often (**cry swim rich**).

If you go to the zoo you may see a (**letter monkey smell**).

A (**spring ticket rabbit**) is an animal with long ears and soft fur.

16

Brilliant Publications
This page may be reproduced by the original purchaser for non-commercial classroom use.

Timely Tasks for Fast Finishers 5–7 Year Olds
© Blake Publishing

Rhyme time

Which rhyming word is correct?
Write it in the space to complete each sentence.

1. **sun**
   gun

   The _____ is shining in the sky.

2. **bat**
   cat

   I saw our _____ catch a mouse.

3. **peg**
   leg

   Tom fell and hurt his _____.

4. **big**
   fig

   An elephant is a _____ animal.

5. **dry**
   fry

   Dad will _____ the fish in the hot oil.

5 MINUTES

Make a sentence

Write the first letter of the name of each object or animal shown in these pictures to make some words. (We have done the first one for you.) All the words together make a sentence. What is it?

A
____

____

____

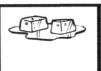
____

____

____

____

____

____

____

____

____

5 MINUTES

ENGLISH

Colour the words

Look at the words in the grid. Colour the names of **toys red**, <u>birds yellow</u> and all the other *animals blue*.

magpie	zebra	top
bat	ball	horse
tiger	hawk	doll
swan	crow	penguin
pig	kite	mouse

There is a trick in this.

One of the toys is also an animal.

Which one is it?_____

Another of the toys is also a bird.

Which one is it?_____

Box on

How many words can you make using the letters in the grid?

Start with a letter or letter pair in the first column. Then use a letter from the second column. Finish the word with a letter or letter pair from the last column.

f	a	sh
th	e	n
sh	i	d
w	u	s

shed ? wish tap chilp shamp fap ?

Brilliant Publications

Timely Tasks for Fast Finishers 5–7 Year Olds

Drop a letter

In each word, cross out a letter to make a new word that matches the picture.

meat

carve

_____

_____

train

broom

_____

_____

wheel

dong

_____

_____

5 MINUTES

Jumblies

Unjumble the letters to make the word that matches the picture. Be careful – you can make more than one word from each.

plma

trsa

_____

_____

hspi

olpo

_____

_____

epa

swa

_____

_____

5 MINUTES

Sssssssss

Circle all the objects in the picture that begin with s.

3 MINUTES

ENGLISH

Changing letters

Change the last letter in each word to make a new word that matches the picture.

 crowd

 food

 mood

 sheen

_____   _____   _____   _____

 bald

 wool

 wine

 carp

_____   _____   _____   _____

5 MINUTES

First letters

Choose the correct letter pair in the brackets to make the word that matches each picture. The first one is done for you.

 __sh__ ip (sh sc)	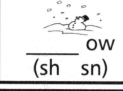 ____ ow (sh sn)	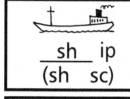 ____ im (sw sk)
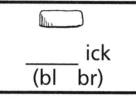 ____ ake (sn st)	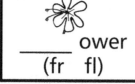 ____ ower (fr fl)	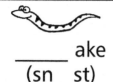 ____ ick (bl br)
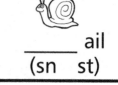 ____ oe (sh st)	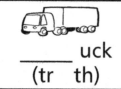 ____ uck (tr th)	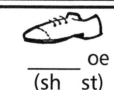 ____ ail (sn st)

5 MINUTES

Brilliant Publications

This page may be reproduced by the original purchaser for non-commercial classroom use.

Timely Tasks for Fast Finishers 5–7 Year Olds

© Blake Publishing

ENGLISH

Small words

Look at the small words in the box.

Add the correct small word to the letters below to make the word that matches each picture.

eat	lag	tar	art
now	oat	old	our

1. s_____

5. g_____

2. m_____

6. c_____

3. f_____

7. f_____

4. c_____

8. s_____

ENGLISH

5 MINUTES

Brilliant Publications

This page may be reproduced by the original purchaser for non-commercial classroom use.

Timely Tasks for Fast Finishers 5–7 Year Olds
© Blake Publishing

21

Write each word backwards and draw a picture of the new word. For example: pat = tap

Use a separate sheet if you need more space for your drawings.

ten _____

nip _____

god _____

tops _____

tar _____

pets _____

but _____

reed _____

Brilliant Publications

Timely Tasks for Fast Finishers 5–7 Year Olds

ENGLISH

Letter pairs

Add **ee** or *oo* in the spaces below to make the words that match the pictures.

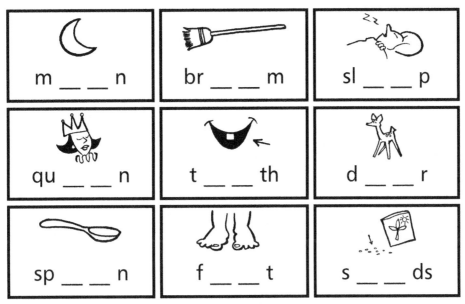

m _ _ n   br _ _ m   sl _ _ p

qu _ _ n   t _ _ th   d _ _ r

sp _ _ n   f _ _ t   s _ _ ds

5 MINUTES

Which word?

Circle the correct answer to each question. Then draw pictures of the answers on a separate sheet.

1. Which one is an insect?   **cup bee dog**

2. Which one is a fruit?   **carrot tiger banana**

3. Which one is a flower?   **rose book can**

4. Which one is an animal?   **pencil zebra tree**

5. Which one is a vegetable?   **carrot bottle paper**

10 MINUTES

ENGLISH

Brilliant Publications

This page may be reproduced by the original purchaser for non-commercial classroom use.

Timely Tasks for Fast Finishers 5–7 Year Olds

© Blake Publishing

23

Parts of something

All the words below are part of something larger.
In the boxes draw what you think each thing is.

floor
ceiling
door
walls

handlebars
wheels
spokes
pedals

leaves
branch
bark
roots
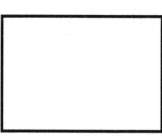

feathers
wing
tail
beak

Nursery rhyme time

Draw a line to connect the parts of these nursery rhymes.
Then draw a picture of one of the rhymes on a separate sheet.

Jack and Jill   runs through the town

Ding dong bell   three men in a tub

Rub-a-dub-dub   sat on a wall

Wee Willie Winkie   come blow your horn

Little Boy Blue   went up the hill

Humpty Dumpty   has lost her sheep

Little Bo Peep   pussy's in the well

ENGLISH

Brilliant Publications
This page may be reproduced by the original purchaser for non-commercial classroom use.

Timely Tasks for Fast Finishers 5–7 Year Olds
© Blake Publishing

Same answers

Work out the number sentences below and write in the answers. The same answer will appear at least three times. Colour each group of rectangles with the same answer in the same colour. You will have to use eight different colours.

5 + 5 =	3 x 3 =	4 x 2 =	8 + 2 =	12 – 3 =
4 x 5 =	10 + 2 =	2 x 2 =	10 + 4 =	9 + 3 =
10 – 4 =	8 – 4 =	10 + 10 =	12 – 6 =	10 – 2 =
5 + 4 =	13 – 4 =	6 + 6 =	2 x 10 =	2 x 7 =
6 + 2 =	6 + 4 =	10 – 6 =	4 + 2 =	13 + 1 =

One of the answers appears four times.

It is the number _____.

Which puppies?

The mother dog has just had six puppies. All her puppies have even numbers and are less than 25.

Colour in only the puppies that belong to the mother dog.

Brilliant Publications

This page may be reproduced by the original purchaser for non-commercial classroom use.

Timely Tasks for Fast Finishers 5–7 Year Olds
© Blake Publishing

MATHS

25

Odds and evens

1. Colour *blue* all the balloons which have an *odd* number for an answer.

2. Colour **red** all balloons with an **even** answer.

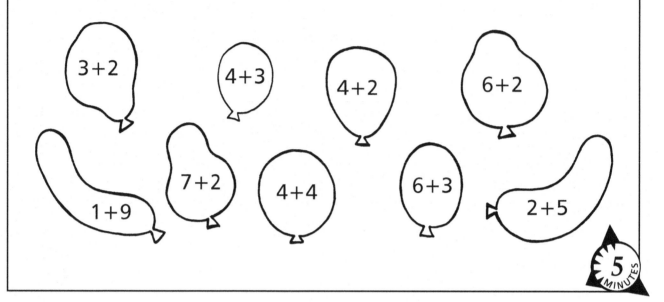

Right and wrong

1. Colour *green* the leaves with a *correct* answer.
2. Colour **brown** those that have a **wrong** answer.

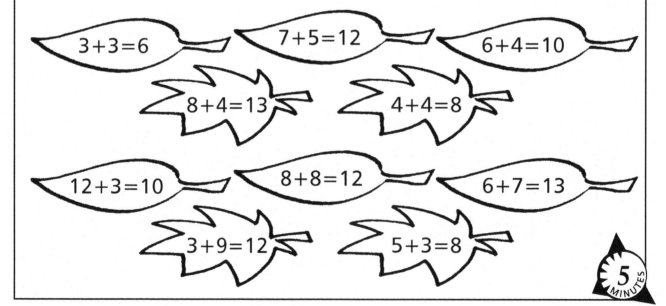

MATHS

Brilliant Publications

This page may be reproduced by the original purchaser for non-commercial classroom use.

Timely Tasks for Fast Finishers 5–7 Year Olds

© Blake Publishing

Picture this

There are a number of different types of things shown in this picture.

How many of each different thing can you see?

Count them and write the numbers in the boxes.

Brilliant Publications

This page may be reproduced by the original purchaser for non-commercial classroom use.

Timely Tasks for Fast Finishers 5–7 Year Olds

© Blake Publishing

27

MATHS

Whose balloons?

Toni, Sally and Mika bought some balloons but they became mixed up.

Toni's balloons have even numbers less than 20.

Sally's balloons have odd numbers less than 20.

Mika's balloons all have numbers more than 20.

Colour *Toni's* balloons *red*, **Sally's yellow** and <u>Mika's blue</u>.

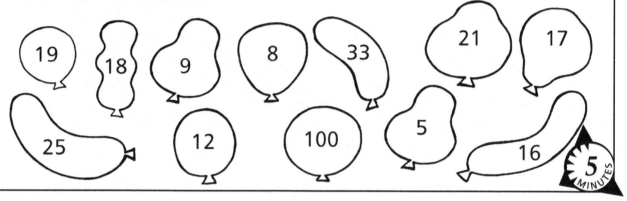

Shape search △

Look closely at the picture. Count all the triangles.

There are_____triangles.

Shape search ☐

Look closely at the picture. Count all the squares.

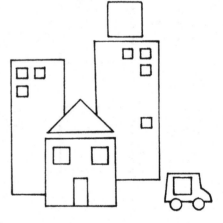

There are_____squares.

MATHS

Brilliant Publications

Timely Tasks for Fast Finishers 5–7 Year Olds
© Blake Publishing

Missing numbers

Write in the missing numbers in each square:

1	2	3
	5	6
7	8	9

1	3	5
7		11
13	15	17

2	4	6
8	10	
14	16	18

5	10	15
20	25	
35	40	45

20	18	16
14		10
8	6	4

1	4	7
10	13	16
19	21	

Position

Circle the picture which is in the position shown at the beginning of each row.

5th	
8th	
6th	
3rd	
4th	
9th	

MATHS

Brilliant Publications

This page may be reproduced by the original purchaser for non-commercial classroom use.

Timely Tasks for Fast Finishers 5–7 Year Olds

© Blake Publishing

29

Maths machine 1

When the mad professor fed the number ⬚6 into the machine it came out as ⬚10. What were the results when he fed the other numbers in?

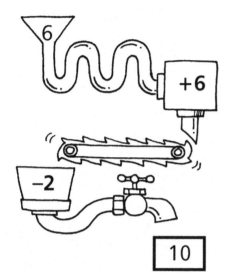

(a) 4 _____   (b) 10 _____

(c) 3 _____   (d) 20 _____

(e) 12 _____   (f) 15 _____

(g) 30 _____   (h) 18 _____

Maths machine 2

Here is another professor's maths machine. When it was fed ⬚4 it came out as ⬚14. What were the results when she fed in the other numbers?

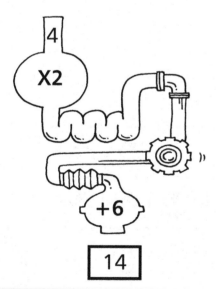

(a) 2 _____   (b) 3 _____

(c) 5 _____   (d) 10 _____

(e) 6 _____   (f) 7 _____

(g) 8 _____   (h) 18 _____

MATHS

Brilliant Publications

This page may be reproduced by the original purchaser for non-commercial classroom use.

Timely Tasks for Fast Finishers 5–7 Year Olds

© Blake Publishing

Half a picture

1. Draw in the missing part of the picture using the grid to help you.

2. Colour in the whole picture.

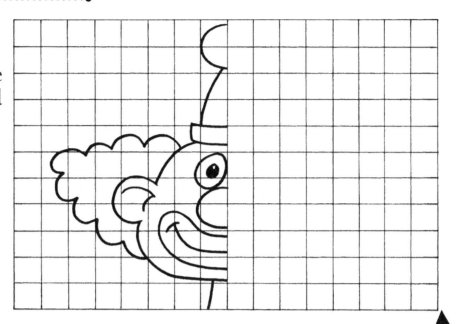

10 MINUTES

Completing patterns

Draw the shape you think comes next.

○ ○ □ □ △ △ ○ ○ □ □ _____

△ □ ▽ ○ △ □ ▽ ○ _____

△ ▽ △ ▽ △ ▽ △ ▽ _____

⋀ ○ △ □ ⋀ ○ △ □ _____

⬭ ○ △ ○ ⧏ □ ⬭ △ ○ _____

5 MINUTES

MATHS

Brilliant Publications

This page may be reproduced by the original purchaser for non-commercial classroom use.

Timely Tasks for Fast Finishers 5–7 Year Olds

© Blake Publishing

31

Colour in 1

Work out the sums in the rectangles. Then use the colour code below to colour the rectangles in the correct colour.

3 = blue   8 = green   4 = red
6 = yellow   7 = pink   5 = black

16–10 =	12–6 =	10–5 =	2+2 =	20–15 =
4+4 =	10–7 =	10–3 =	7–4 =	10–2 =
10–4 =	12–8 =	6–3 =	4+3 =	14–10 =
2x3 =	12–7 =	10–6 =	2x4 =	12–4 =

Colour in 2

Work out the sums in the rectangles. Then use the colour code below to colour the rectangles in the correct colour.

10 = blue   12 = green 15 = red
16 = yellow   20 = pink   30 = black

3x4+3 =	2x4+2 =	4x5–5 =	5x3+5 =
3x10–10 =	20–2–2 =	3+9+4+4 =	2x8–6 =
20–10 =	2x6+8 =	4x2+4 =	5x2+20 =
7+4+5 =	2x6–0 =	7+3+5 =	2x10+10 =

MATHS

Brilliant Publications

Timely Tasks for Fast Finishers 5–7 Year Olds
© Blake Publishing

Adding on

In each row draw the extra pictures to make up the number shown.

8	🐕 🐕
6	🍐
10	🍰 🍰 🍰
9	🐞

Shaping up

Colour triangles △ *red*. Colour squares ☐ *blue*. Colour rectangles ▭ *yellow*. Colour circles ○ *green*.

MATHS

Breakfast adding

There are two sausages and one egg for each child. Draw lines linking each sausage and egg to the child who has the correct answer on their plate.

One has been done for you.

Twelve

Each sum has a letter above it. In the empty squares, write all the letters that appear above sums that make 12.

If you do it correctly you will discover the name of a fruit.

o	t	r	a	b	n	g	p	e
6 + 6	3 + 4	6 x 2	3 x 4	10 – 7	8 + 4	10 + 10	7 + 5	9 + 3

The first letter has been put in for you.

| o | | | | | |

Draw the fruit:

MATHS

34

Brilliant Publications
This page may be reproduced by the original purchaser for non-commercial classroom use.

Timely Tasks for Fast Finishers 5–7 Year Olds
© Blake Publishing

Circles

Colour the two numbers that add up to the number in the centre of each circle. The first one has been done for you.

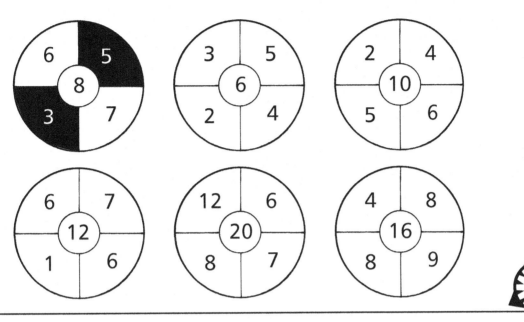

Follow the evens

1. Follow only the lines with even numbers on them.
2. As you follow these lines, you will come across letters.
3. Write these in the boxes below and you will discover the name of an animal. The first letter has been put in for you.

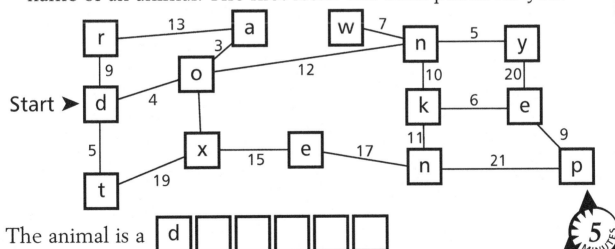

The animal is a d ☐ ☐ ☐ ☐ ☐

MATHS

Square up

Count the number of squares.
Write your answer below.

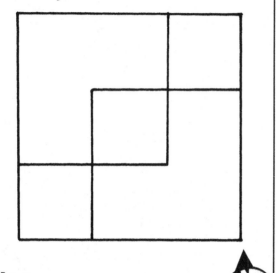

Answer: _____ squares.

(3 MINUTES)

Fish

James catches only fish that have an **odd** number for their answer. Colour them **red**.

Jacqueline catches only fish that have an *even* number for their answer. Colour them *blue*.

3+5   7+2   5+4   8+5   9+3   12−3   10−4   11−3   12−6   7−2

(5 MINUTES)

Kites

Draw a line from each kite to the person with the correct answer. How many kites does each person have?

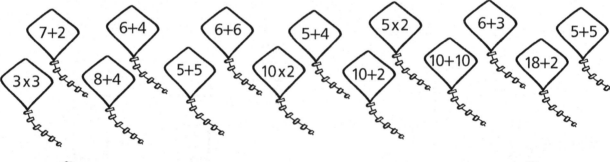

7+2   6+4   6+6   5+4   5x2   6+3   5+5
3x3   8+4   5+5   10x2   10+2   10+10   18+2

12–Zoe   9–Jodie   20–Tim   10–Meg

Zoe has___kites. Jodie has___kites. Tim has___kites. Meg has___kites.

 (5 MINUTES)

MATHS

Brilliant Publications

Timely Tasks for Fast Finishers 5–7 Year Olds
© Blake Publishing

Flower arrangements

Draw lines between the flower sums and the vases that belong together.

Each vase has two flowers.

Fishy tales

All the fish Tommy caught have the correct answer on them.
Colour the fish that Tommy caught.

Brilliant Publications

This page may be reproduced by the original purchaser for non-commercial classroom use.

Timely Tasks for Fast Finishers 5–7 Year Olds
© Blake Publishing

37

MATHS

Ordering

Colour the row of balls following the instructions below.

1st

1. Colour the third ball yellow.

2. Colour the fifth ball pink.

3. Colour the second ball brown.

4. Colour the fourth ball blue.

10 MINUTES

Shapes

Colour all **squares blue**.
Colour all *triangles yellow*.
Colour all <u>rectangles green</u>.
Colour all ***circles red***.

5 MINUTES

Get ready

The cars are ready to begin the race.

Before they can start you must find the number to put in the back wheel so both wheels add up to the number on the car.

5 MINUTES

MATHS

Brilliant Publications

Timely Tasks for Fast Finishers 5–7 Year Olds

© Blake Publishing

Pathways

Colour red the two's path through the grid to reach 48. To do this, keep counting by 2.

All the coloured boxes must be touching, either at the side, top, bottom or corner.

Now colour blue the three's path to 48. To do this, keep counting by 3.

8	3	**2**	0	4	8	40	**3**	99	21
5	9	7	4	11	48	21	6	8	14
11	12	8	6	46	9	12	9	7	11
3	6	41	8	44	7	15	3	6	9
7	9	10	21	16	42	18	21	9	8
16	14	12	22	13	40	7	24	27	48
18	12	11	23	36	38	6	7	30	45
20	13	20	5	34	6	5	9	33	42
14	22	24	7	32	5	8	8	36	39
15	18	26	28	30	4	3	11	6	7
16	17	19	9	11	0	11	4	5	6

MATHS

Brilliant Publications

This page may be reproduced by the original purchaser for non-commercial classroom use.

Timely Tasks for Fast Finishers 5–7 Year Olds

© Blake Publishing

39

Work out each number fact.
Then find the answer in the grid and colour it as instructed.

1. 3 + 3 + 6 = ____ brown

2. 7 – 3 – 3 = ____ red

3. 5 x 2 + 6 = ____ yellow

4. 10 + 10 = ____ green

5. 4 + 5 + 6 = ____ dark blue

6. 3 x 3 = ____ light blue

20	4	11	5	3
8	7	9	12	6
18	16	15	14	10
1	2	30	100	50

5 MINUTES

What socks?

Can you find the matching socks?
They are socks that have exactly the same answers.
Colour each pair of socks the same colour.

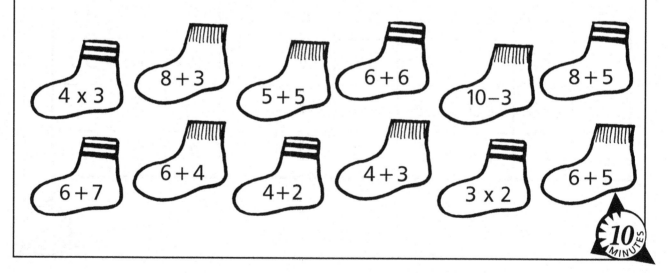

MAThS

10 MINUTES

Brilliant Publications

Timely Tasks for Fast Finishers 5–7 Year Olds
© Blake Publishing

Number maze

Work out the number facts below:

1. 3 + 3 = _____   2. 3 + 2 = _____   3. 4 + 4 = _____

4. 6 + 3 = _____   5. 5 + 5 = _____   6. 7 + 7 = _____

7. 6 + 5 = _____

Now follow the answers to these sums to get through the maze, starting with the answer to number 1.

Each number has a letter at the beginning of its line. Write the letters in the boxes below to make the name of something you might use at school or home.

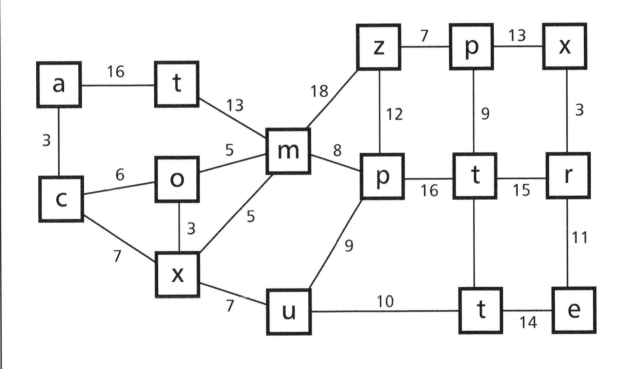

Brilliant Publications

This page may be reproduced by the original purchaser for non-commercial classroom use.

Timely Tasks for Fast Finishers 5–7 Year Olds
© Blake Publishing

41

MATHS

Birthdays

Hamid, Sally, Ben and Jacinta all have their birthdays in April.
Read all the clues then write each name next to the correct date.

• Hamid's birthday is in the last week of April.

• Sally's birthday is two weeks after Ben's.

• Ben's birthday is on April Fool's Day.

• 5 + 4 equals Jacinta's birthday.

1. _____ April 1st

2. _____ April 9th

3. _____ April 15th

4. _____ April 28th

It's bananas!

Our class held a banana-eating contest last week.

Using the numbers and the clues below, can you work out how many bananas each person ate? 14, 6, 8, 10, 12.

Name	Bananas
Matthew	
Paul	
Jemima	
Sula	
Mike	

1. Jemima ate the most bananas.

2. Sula ate the least number of bananas.

3. Matthew ate the second highest number of bananas.

4. Mike ate two bananas less than Matthew.

5. Paul ate two more bananas than Sula.

Brilliant Publications
Timely Tasks for Fast Finishers 5–7 Year Olds
© Blake Publishing

MATHS

Colour by number

Work out the sums in the box to find out what colour to use for each shape. Now colour the picture using the colour code.

- 8 orange
- 12 blue
- 16 brown
- 20 light green
- 15 dark green

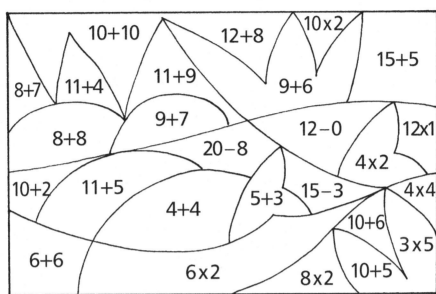

Number sentences

How many number sentences can you make to equal 8?
Use the numbers in the boxes and the signs +, −, x and ÷.
One has been done for you.   6 + 2 = 8

4	2	
1	6	8
7	3	10	5

Use a separate sheet to write out your number sentences.

Brilliant Publications
This page may be reproduced by the original purchaser for non-commercial classroom use.

Timely Tasks for Fast Finishers 5–7 Year Olds
© Blake Publishing

43

MATHS

Colour this picture using as many colours as you wish but making sure no areas of the same colour touch each other.

THINKING

10 MINUTES

Careful colour

Colour this design using only three colours and making sure that no shapes of the same colour touch each other.

Colour design

Colour in the shapes below any way you wish to make an attractive design.

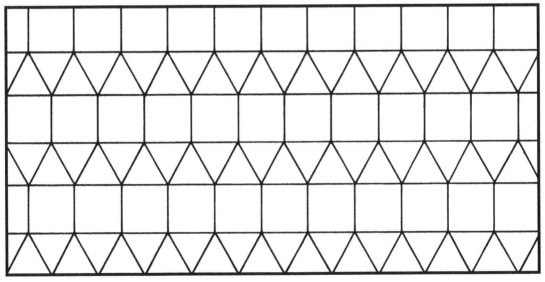

THINKING

Brilliant Publications

This page may be reproduced by the original purchaser for non-commercial classroom use.

Timely Tasks for Fast Finishers 5–7 Year Olds
© Blake Publishing

45

Look at the picture pairs below. If the two pictures are the same, colour them red. If they are different, colour one red and one blue.

THINKING

Brilliant Publications
This page may be reproduced by the original purchaser for non-commercial classroom use.

Timely Tasks for Fast Finishers 5–7 Year Olds
© Blake Publishing

Spot the error

Find the mistake in each picture.
Put a cross over it.

Match up

Draw lines to join the socks that make a pair.
Colour the pairs the same colour.

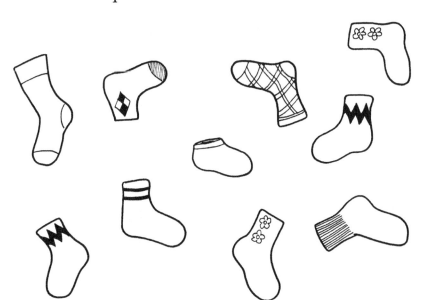 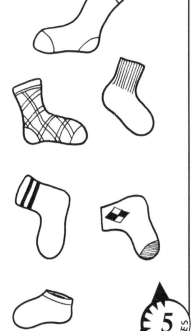

Brilliant Publications
This page may be reproduced by the original purchaser for non-commercial classroom use.

Timely Tasks for Fast Finishers 5–7 Year Olds
© Blake Publishing

47

THINKING

Look how A has changed to B.

Now look at C.

C

Which shape would C change to in the same way?

The answer is: .

Now try these patterns. Circle the correct shape in each row.

1.	A B	C	
2.	A B	C	
3.	A B	C	
4.	 A B	C	
5.	A B	C	
6.	A B	C	

THINKING

Brilliant Publications

5 MINUTES

Shadow play

Draw lines to match the shadow picture pairs that go together.

Out of place

Circle the picture in each row that is different from the others.
Colour all the pictures.

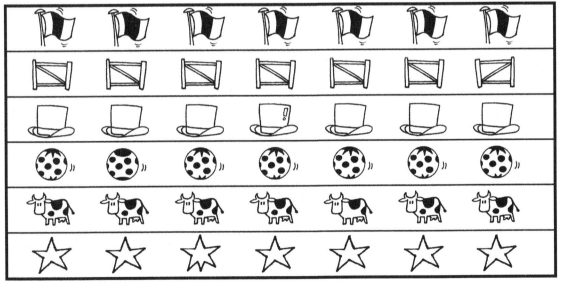

THINKING

Brilliant Publications

This page may be reproduced by the original purchaser for non-commercial classroom use.

Timely Tasks for Fast Finishers 5–7 Year Olds
© Blake Publishing

49

Colour the two pictures in each box that are the same.

THINKING

5 MINUTES

Add on

Add the missing pieces to the second picture in each pair.

Left and right

Match each picture on the left with its partner on the right.

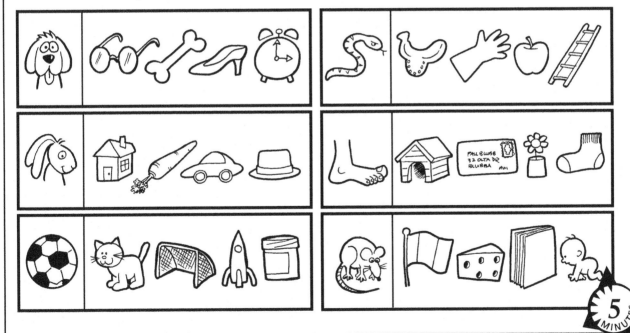

Brilliant Publications

THINKING

Timely Tasks for Fast Finishers 5–7 Year Olds

© Blake Publishing

A beautiful scene is hidden in the shapes below.

Colour the shapes marked: **BL in blue, O in orange, P in purple, G in green, DG in dark green, Y in yellow and BR in brown.**

THINKING

52

Brilliant Publications

This page may be reproduced by the original purchaser for non-commercial classroom use.

Timely Tasks for Fast Finishers 5–7 Year Olds

© Blake Publishing

What comes next?

Colour the first three shapes and then the shape that comes next in the pattern. Use the same colour in a row.

1.
2.
3.
4.
5.

What happened?

Look at the pictures on the left. What happened next? Draw a line to match the picture pairs.

THINKING

THINKING

Brilliant Publications

This page may be reproduced by the original purchaser for non-commercial classroom use.

Timely Tasks for Fast Finishers 5–7 Year Olds
© Blake Publishing

53

1. Draw a black horse under the tree.
2. Draw five sheep in the far field.
3. Draw two birds in the tree.
4. Draw two eggs in the bird's nest.
5. Draw a man rowing a boat.

THINKING

54

Brilliant Publications

This page may be reproduced by the original purchaser for non-commercial classroom use.

Timely Tasks for Fast Finishers 5–7 Year Olds

© Blake Publishing

Copy cats

Copy the lines on the left onto the dots on the right.
The first one is done for you.

1.

2.

3.

4.

5.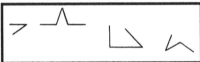

6.

What's missing?

Circle the piece in each box that best completes the shapes.

1.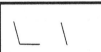

2.

3.

4.

5.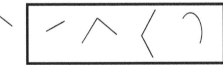

6.

THINKING

Brilliant Publications

This page may be reproduced by the original purchaser for non-commercial classroom use.

Timely Tasks for Fast Finishers 5–7 Year Olds

© Blake Publishing

55

The same

Look at the shapes in the box. Colour each one a different colour.
Now find its partner outside the box and colour it to match.

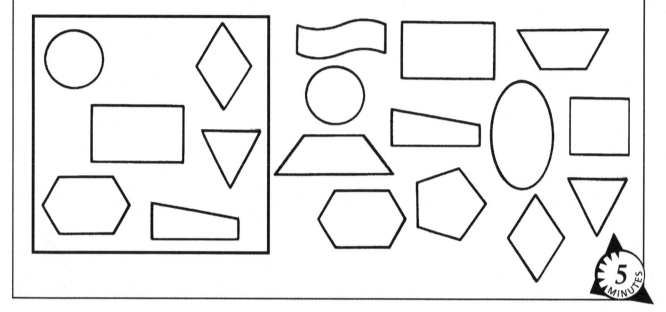

Colour in

Using any colours, shade each of these designs exactly the same as the smaller design below.

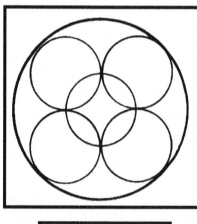
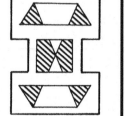
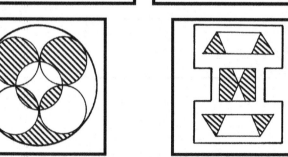

THINKING

Brilliant Publications

Timely Tasks for Fast Finishers 5–7 Year Olds
© Blake Publishing

Inside and outside

Colour *red* those things you would find *inside* your home.
Colour *yellow* those things you would find *outside* your home.

Picture puzzle

Look closely at the two pictures. In the second one a number of changes have been made. Put a cross over the changes. How many did you find?

Brilliant Publications

This page may be reproduced by the original purchaser for non-commercial classroom use.

Timely Tasks for Fast Finishers 5–7 Year Olds
© Blake Publishing

57

THINKING

Pet puzzler

Amal's parents gave her a pet for her birthday. Can you tell which pet they gave her?

- It doesn't have fur.
- It doesn't eat meat.
- It cannot fly.

Colour Amal's pet.

Picture this

Look at this picture carefully. Put a cross over all the things that are wrong.

THINKING

58

Brilliant Publications
This page may be reproduced by the original purchaser for non-commercial classroom use.

Timely Tasks for Fast Finishers 5–7 Year Olds
© Blake Publishing

Shaping the puzzle

Find the shape by reading the clues below and colour it in.

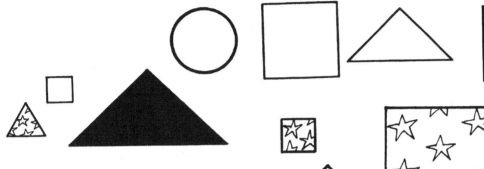

1. It does not have stars.
2. It is not dark.
3. It is smaller than the circle.
4. It has only three sides.

In the past

The pictures below show something that was used in the past. In the box beside each one, draw a picture of what we use today instead.

Use a separate sheet for your drawings if you need more space.

THINKING

Brilliant Publications
This page may be reproduced by the original purchaser for non-commercial classroom use.

Timely Tasks for Fast Finishers 5–7 Year Olds
© Blake Publishing

59

Someone began this picture, but didn't get time to finish it. Can you finish it?

Colouring in

Colour the pattern below any way you wish to make an attractive design.

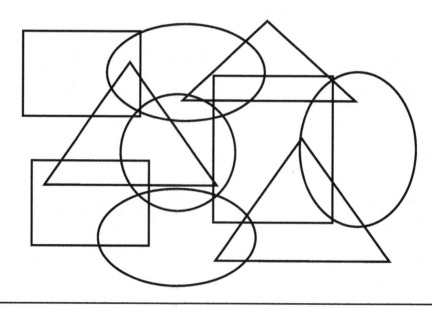

THINKING

Brilliant Publications

© Blake Publishing

Electricity

Look at the picture. Put a cross over all the things that are dangerous.

Magnets

Colour the things that a magnet would pick up.

Brilliant Publications

This page may be reproduced by the original purchaser for non-commercial classroom use.

Timely Tasks for Fast Finishers 5–7 Year Olds
© Blake Publishing

61

SCIENCE

These children are having trouble pushing the box across the room. What would you suggest to help them? Draw what you would do.

62 Brilliant Publications

This page may be reproduced by the original purchaser for non-commercial classroom use.

Timely Tasks for Fast Finishers 5–7 Year Olds

© Blake Publishing

Power

Colour the things that need electricity to work.

Day & night

Colour this picture as daytime.   Colour this picture as night-time.

SCIENCE

Cut out the pictures and paste them on a sheet in the order they would happen.

SCIENCE

Summer & winter

Look at the pictures. Show whether they belong in winter or summer by drawing these symbols in the squares.

The symbol for **winter** is

The symbol for *summer* is

In these boxes draw what you like to do in each season.

Brilliant Publications

This page may be reproduced by the original purchaser for non-commercial classroom use.

Timely Tasks for Fast Finishers 5–7 Year Olds
© Blake Publishing

65

SCIENCE

Cut out these pictures and paste them on a sheet in the order they would happen.

Living things

Circle the living things pictured below.

Brilliant Publications

66

This page may be reproduced by the original purchaser for non-commercial classroom use.

Timely Tasks for Fast Finishers 5–7 Year Olds

© Blake Publishing

Families

Here are some pictures of family members helping around the home. What is missing in each one? Draw it and then colour the pictures.

PSHE

5 MINUTES

Look at these pictures. Use the words below to complete the sentences about them.

carrying   drying   digging   mowing

1. Susan is _____ in the garden.
2. Mike is _____ the dishes.
3. Tom is _____ the heavy bag.
4. Tuki is _____ the lawn.

5 MINUTES

Find the food words in the grid. Write each one under its matching picture.

M	E	A	T	B	B
M	I	L	K	R	U
E	P	S	F	E	T
G	E	A	I	A	T
G	A	L	S	D	E
S	S	T	H	X	R

_____   _____   _____

_____   _____   _____

_____   _____

10 MINUTES

PSHE

Timely Tasks for Fast Finishers 5–7 Year Olds
© Blake Publishing

English

Page 4
Make a word
1. sun
2. peg
3. tap
4. pen
5. dog

Change the order
rat

arm

tap

saw

ten

ant

Little words
hen

egg

car

rat

pan

rain

owl

Page 5
Wordsearch
cow

pig

horse

bear

rabbit

dog

tiger

What's there?
The following are not found in the picture and therefore should not be coloured in: book, cow, chair, elephant, house, plate, ball, cup

Page 6
Fill in the gaps
clown

crown

snow

bowl

town

Picture this
fox

box

top

mat

fan

mop

Classifying
Things to eat—cake, butter, pizza

Things to play—cricket, games, football

Things to wear—shoes, hat, jumper

Page 7
Jumbled up
ball

nest

ship

star

lock

drum

Page 8
Picture this
1. Yes
2. No
3. No
4. Yes
5. Yes
6. Yes

Find my name
1. pig
2. bed

Page 10
Rhyme time
Jack and Jill went up the hill

To fetch a pail of water.

Jack fell down and broke his crown

And Jill came tumbling after.

Mary had a little lamb,

Its fleece was white as snow.

And everywhere that Mary went

The lamb was sure to go.

Word pictures
duck, pond, dog, cat, duck, nest, nest, eggs, snake, hole, duck

Page 11
How many?
Red—chair, pig, goat, dog, tiger, zebra, cat, table

Yellow—girl, boy, goose, lady, hen, owl, duck, man

Changing letters
pool

card

pear

cake

goat

rain

milk

wing

duck

Page 12
Otters
1. Yes
2. No
3. Yes
4. No
5. Colour it brown

Page 13
Which word?
1. lemon
2. wool
3. garden
4. pencil
5. tiger
6. bucket

Crosswords
→
1. boat

↓
1. bone
2. tent

→
1. four
4. egg

↓
2. one
3. rugs

→
2. ship
3. flag

↓
1. hill

→
2. teeth

↓
1. tears
3. train

Page 14
Woodpeckers
1. True
2. False
3. False
4. True

Page 15
Fill in the gaps
sail

rain

train

chain

nail

tail

snail

brain

Make it up
fox, cup, bat, bed

Making words
Cat, can, cap, car, bat, bin, bag, bun

Page 16
Add a letter
gold

star

wing

drum

ship

flag

wheel

broom

Which word?
milk   monkey

tent   rabbit

cry

Brilliant Publications

This page may be reproduced by the original purchaser for non-commercial classroom use.

Timely Tasks for Fast Finishers 5–7 Year Olds
© Blake Publishing

69

ANSWERS

Page 17
Rhyme time
1. sun
2. cat
3. leg
4. big
5. fry

Make a sentence
A big dog bit me.

Page 18
Colour the words
Red: toys – top, ball, bat, doll, kite

Blue: animals – zebra, bat, horse, tiger, pig, mouse

Yellow: birds – magpie, swan, hawk, crow, penguin, kite

A bat is a toy and an animal.

A kite is a toy and a bird.

Box on
Fad, fan, fed, fen, fin, fish, fun, than, then, thin, this, thud, thus, shed, shin, shun, shush, wad, wan, was, wash, wed, win, wish.

Page 19
Drop a letter
mat
rain
heel
cave
room
dog

Jumblies
lamp   star
ship   pool
pea   saw

Sssssssss

sun, sail, shade, shower, spade, snail, shells, surf, swimmer, stairs, singer,

seats, sand castle, sea, store

Page 20
Changing letters
crown
foot
moon
sheep
ball
wood
wind
card

First letters
sh ship
sn snow
sw swim
sn snake
fl flower
br brick
sh shoe
tr truck
sn snail

Page 21
Small words
1. snow
2. meat
3. flag
4. cart
5. gold
6 coat
7. four
8. star

Page 22
Back to front
ten/net
nip/pin
god/dog
tops/spot
tar/rat
pets/step
but/tub
reed/deer

Page 23
Letter pairs
moon   deer
broom   spoon
sleep   feet
queen   seeds
tooth

Which word?
1. bee
2. banana
3. rose
4. zebra
5. carrot

Page 24
Parts of something
Room, bicycle, tree, bird

Nursery rhyme time
Jack and Jill went up the hill.

Ding dong bell pussy's in the well.

Rub-a-dub-dub three men in a tub.

Wee Willie Winkie runs through the town.

Little Boy Blue come blow your horn.

Humpty Dumpty sat on a wall.

Little Bo Peep has lost her sheep.

Maths
Page 25
Same answers
Answers are grouped thus:

4   2 x 2, 8 – 4, 10 – 6

6   10 – 4, 12 – 6, 4 + 2

8   4 x 2, 10 – 2, 6 + 2

9   3 x 3, 12 – 3, 5 + 4, 13 – 4 (9 appears 4 times)

10   5 + 5, 8 + 2, 6 + 4

12   10 + 2, 9 + 3, 6 + 6

14   10 + 4, 2 x 7, 13 + 1

20   4 x 5, 10 + 10, 2 x 10

Which puppies?
12, 6, 18, 24, 20, 16

Page 26
Odds and evens
Blue—3+2, 4+3, 7+2, 6+3, 2+5

Red—4+2, 6+2, 1+9, 4+4

Right and wrong
Green—3+3, 7+5, 6+4, 4+4, 6+7, 3+9, 5+3

Brown—8+4, 12+3, 8+8

Page 27
Picture this
birds—2
sheep—4
pigs—2
cats—1
dogs—3
trees—9
flowers—5
people—5
ducks—6

Page 28
Whose balloons?
Toni: 18, 8, 12, 16
Sally: 19, 9, 17, 5
Mika: 33, 21, 25, 100

Shape search – triangle
19

Shape search – square
12

Page 29
Missing numbers
4
9
12
30
12
24

70

Brilliant Publications

This page may be reproduced by the original purchaser for non-commercial classroom use.

Timely Tasks for Fast Finishers 5–7 Year Olds

© Blake Publishing

ANSWERS

Page 30
Maths machine 1
+6 −2
a) 8
b) 14
c) 7
d) 24
e) 16
f) 19
g) 34
h) 22

Maths machine 2
x2 +6
a) 10
b) 12
c) 16
d) 26
e) 18
f) 20
g) 22
h) 42

Page 31
Completing patterns

Page 32
Colour in 1
3: blue
10 − 7, 7 − 4, 6 − 3
8: green
4 + 4, 10 − 2, 2 x 4,
12 − 4
4: red
2 + 2, 12 − 8, 14 − 10,
10 − 6
6: yellow
16 − 10, 12 − 6,
10 − 4, 2 x 3

7: pink
10 − 3, 4 + 3,
5: black
10 − 5, 20 − 15, 12 − 7

Colour in 2
10: blue
2 x 4 + 2, 2 x 8 − 6,
20 − 10
12: green
4 x 2 + 4, 2 x 6 − 0,
15: red
3 x 4 + 3, 4 x 5 − 5,
7 + 3 + 5,
16: yellow
20 − 2 − 2, 7 + 4 + 5
20: pink
5 x 3 + 5, 3 x 10 − 10,
3 + 9 + 4 + 4, 2 x 6 + 8
30: black
2 x 10 + 10, 5 x 2 + 20

Page 34
Breakfast adding
12: 15 − 3, 6 + 6, 7 + 5
8: 10 − 2, 5 + 3, 4 x 2
14: 9 + 5, 7 x 2, 8 + 6

Twelve
Orange

Page 35
Circles
5 + 3, 2 + 4,
4 + 6, 6 + 6,
12 + 8, 8 + 8

Follow the evens
Donkey

Page 36
Square up
6

Fish
James
7 + 2
5 + 4
8 + 5
12 − 3
7 − 2

Jacqueline
3 + 5
9 + 3
10 − 4
12 − 6
11 − 3

Kites
Zoe has 3 kites.
Tim has 3 kites.
Jodie has 4 kites.
Meg has 4 kites.

Page 37
Flower arrangements
Vase	Flowers
12	6 x 2, 6 + 6
10	5 + 5, 6 + 4
20	15 + 5, 10 + 10
8	4 + 4, 4 x 2

Fishy tales
Tommy has caught 6 fish:
6 + 4 = 10
9 + 3 = 12
12 − 3 = 9
10 − 4 = 6
8 − 5 = 3
14 − 4 = 10

Page 38
Get ready
7 + 5 = 12
11 + 9 = 20
8 + 8 = 16
9 + 5 = 14
7 + 6 = 13
6 + 5 = 11

Page 39
Pathways

8	3	**2**	0	4	8	40	**3**	99	21
5	9	7	4	11	48	21	6	8	14
11	12	8	6	46	9	12	9	7	11
3	6	41	8	44	7	15	3	6	9
7	9	10	21	16	42	18	21	9	8
16	14	12	22	13	40	7	24	27	48
18	12	11	23	36	38	6	7	30	45
20	13	20	5	34	6	5	9	33	42
14	22	24	7	32	5	8	8	36	39
15	18	26	28	30	4	3	11	6	7
16	17	19	9	11	0	11	4	5	6

Page 40
Answer box
12 − brown
1 − red
16 − yellow
20 − green
15 − dark blue
9 − light blue

What socks?
Pairs:
4 x 3 and 6 + 6
8 + 3 and 6 + 5
5 + 5 and 6 + 4
10 − 3 and 4 + 3
8 + 5 and 6 + 7
4 + 2 and 3 x 2

Page 41
Number maze
computer

Page 42
Birthdays
1. Ben − April 1st
2. Jacinta − April 9th
3. Sally − April 15th
4. Hamid − April 28th

It's bananas!
Matthew − 12
Paul − 8
Jemima − 14
Sula − 6
Mike − 10

Brilliant Publications

This page may be reproduced by the original purchaser for non-commercial classroom use.

Timely Tasks for Fast Finishers 5–7 Year Olds
© Blake Publishing

71

ANSWERS

Page 43
Number sentences
4 x 2

4 + 1 + 3

7 + 1

10 − 2

10 − 5 + 3

3 + 5

6 + 3 − 1

You will find lots more!

Thinking

Page 46
Match up
Colour red:
Circles, cones, flags, houses, flowers, hats

Colour red and blue:
Horses, nails, chimneys, robots, mice, building

Page 47
Spot the error
The plug should be plugged into the socket.

The horses have no bridles.

Page 48
Changes
1. small white square
2. small white hexagon
3. large black hexagon
4. small white star
5. small white hexagon
6. large black star

Page 49
Shadow play
Door/key

Car/wheel

Knife/fork

Flower/pot

Water/boat

Trunk/elephant

Fire engine/hose

Dog/tail

Rake/shovel

Out of place
Row 1. Second flag

Row 2. Last gate

Row 3. Fourth hat

Row 4. Second ball

Row 5. Fifth cow

Row 6. Third star

Page 51
Left and right
Dog/bone

Snake/apple

Rabbit/carrot

Foot/sock

Football/net

Mouse/cheese

Page 53
What comes next?
1. third shape
2. first shape
3. third shape
4. first shape
5. third shape

What happened?
Oven/biscuits

Alarm clock/brushing teeth

Packing picnic basket/picnic

Cat wanting to be fed/cat eating

Page 55
What's missing?
1. first piece
2. last piece
3. second piece
4. second piece
5. first piece
6. third piece

Page 57
Inside and outside
Inside—television, kettle, bed, bath.

Outside—shovel, tree, swimming pool, hose.

Picture puzzle
10 differences.

Page 58
Pet puzzler
The fish.

Picture this

Page 59
Shaping the puzzle
Small triangle.

Science

Page 61
Electricity

Magnets
Safety pin, nail, needle, sewing pin.

Page 62
Movement
The children could put the rollers under the box and roll it along.

Page 63
Power
Hairdryer, toaster, radio, television, iron.

Page 64
Weather

Page 66
Cooking

Living things
Rat, flower, person, fish, ant.

PSHE

Page 67
Families
Cutting lawn, mower missing.

Painting house, paint brush missing.

Sweeping path, broom missing.

Cutting hedge, shears missing.

Page 68
Helping others
Susan is digging in the garden.

Mike is drying the dishes.

Tom is carrying the heavy bag.

Tuki is mowing the lawn.

Food
meat, bread, butter, milk, peas, fish, eggs, salt

Brilliant Publications

This page may be reproduced by the original purchaser for non-commercial classroom use.

Timely Tasks for Fast Finishers 5–7 Year Olds

© Blake Publishing